PAEANS

A COLLECTION OF READER COMMISSIONED POEMS

FROM
LUKE MAGUIRE ARMSTRONG

Paeans

© 2023 Luke Maguire Armstrong

All Rights Reserved

But go ahead, reproduce in ways known and not. Kinda feels like we aren't talking about copyrights anymore, know what I mean? ;) Reproduce in languages existing and to come. Proclaim what occurs to you as worthy from rooftops. Cite sources. Be careful not to slip or quit. Skip. And hum. Sip slowly, this tea's hot! Have fun.

Oogabooga! Oogabooga! Woofles and waffles!
Biscuits and gravy!
We're as soaring as we're sound.

Cover Photo "Sunflower in the Concrete" by Elizabeth Sparks

Carpe Diem
luke@TravelWriteSing.com
www.TravelWriteSing.com
IG/YouTube: @AuthorLukeMA
FB: Author Luke Maguire Armstrong

Table of Contents

AUTHORS'S NOTE   7

A BODY DRUG FREE   15
MAGIC LEGS   16
STROKE OF LUCK   18
HOW I'LL CARRY YOU   20
ADVICE TO SOMEONE BUILDING A HOUSE   21
MAMA BEARS   23
RESCUE DOGS   24

FORGIVENESS AND RESENTMENT   25
SANDY'S SHORE   27
WHY FORGIVENESS?   29
THINGS TO LOVE ABOUT YOU   30
THE FALL OF FEAR   31
DEPRESSION'S DOOR   32
MY SMILE   34

A FALLEN TOWER   35
THE HAPPY BIRTHDAY EXPRESS   36
WHAT MAKES ME SMILE   37
THE RIPENING OF THE SOUL   39
SEA MOTHER   40
LOVE AT FIRST SIGHT   41
HATS   42

DARKNESS AS A DOORWAY   43
FINDING YOUR EMAHO   44
THEIR VOICE   45

THE MOUNTAIN'S GAZE   46
HOW TO BE AT PEACE IN THE WORLD   47
FAITH. DOUBT. AND COURAGE IN MEDITATION   48
SEEING THE SEA   50
BALANCE IN THE CHAOS   51
INDECISION   52
GROUND CONTROL TO DAVID BOWIE   54

LOVE OF LIFE   55
THROUGH A CHILD'S EYE   56
COCOON STAGE   58
ALSO ANXIETY   59
THE NEXT CHAPTER   60
SUNFLOWER IN THE CONCRETE   61
ABOUT THE AUTHOR AND KOKO BEAR   64

Paeans

AUTHOR'S NOTE

paean
noun

pae· an ˈpē-ən , sounds like like "peein'"

1: a joyous song or hymn of praise, tribute, thanksgiving, or triumph
2: a work that praises or honors its subject : encomium, tribute
3: a collection of poetry by Luke Maguire Armstrong

Ex. And upon hearing his parents ride in, Homer stashed the scroll upon which he had been penning a paean to Apollo for being such a cool God and amazing musician and archer and poet and healer and all the stuff that makes Apollo so great!

As Homer told it, the Greek deity Apollo would sometimes take on the appearance of "Paean," healer to the gods.

The earliest musical "paeans" were hymns of praise dedicated to Apollo sung at events ranging from raging festivals to public funerals, to traditional marching songs to armies headed to war. Over time, the word became generalized— now "paeans" is connotative of any kind of tribute. In terms of Apollo's greater significance in the Hellenistic cosmology, he was the fricken man—slayer of pythons, epic break dancer, had the dankest flat bread recipe, and was spoken word poetry wizard. He was the first guy to ever come up with music. Maidens swooned whenever Apollo rolled in with his posse of beatboxing deities!

I first encountered the word "Paeans" in an email from 2008 from my paternal grandmother, poet Patricia Mees Armstrong. I didn't know then that this was her last year on Earth. She left me all of her books in her will, and in the unwritten will of our hearts, she bequeathed me poetry by being a poet and in her final years recognizing me as a peer on that path.

Titling this collection, "Paeans" led for me to search the back corner of my inbox for the email where it was first used. That led me to re-reading and analyzing our electronic correspondence from my new vantage point of now.
From that I met my fifteen years deceased grandma again.

Dead people are still people. And when you continue conversations with those now passed, their life continues in you. In my background context she is this pillar of poetry in my family who had the secret of words alive in her heart as I in mine. Poets understand the task placed in the poet's hand. We are ever grateful to find another carrying the same flame.

From: Luke Armstrong
To: Patricia Mees Armstrong
Subject: Happy Sunday
Date: June, 1 2008

Hi grandma,

I hope you are enjoying your Sunday. I just returned from a hike into the hills surrounding Antigua. It was fabulous. I did not see a single person the whole time. I hiked up high enough to touch the clouds, only to find that once I reached them all they did is turn into a lovely mist to cool the sweat from the hike. On the top of a mountain, my thoughts went to you and I wrote you a poem. I hope maybe I touched upon some of the ageless beauty that you encapsulate. Thanks for being in my life and I hope you enjoy the poem.

Love,
Luke

Enslosure:
Seaside Grace

SEASIDE GRACE

In Memory of Patricia Mees Armstrong

like post orgasmic peace, the living waves, slaves to you not
so neutral moon, slave to earth, home to you, admired
waves; a green, ripe opening, unlit fires of
night, hazy inspiration, not so far from
the truth: all ice cubes will one
day be sea-foaming surf,

to be sliced right open, again, water mending wounds;
the hermit crab's home rests between two sea-tanned
breasts, which through a series of perfect parts,
connects to two traveled feet, leaving
hopeless prints on ever washing
sands,

a song of one sound sets tempo in her musical ears,
the washing cleanses what harm it brings,
scores of voices, who have never turned her
down, mix water without words, under
a late-light sky,

so see the orange blued of the set and rise, imagine what's
behind the curtain of a green, silk skirt, and trade a
day to pass away in a moment of minutes,
outside itself, and beside itself, with
Grace.

the fall, the quiet spectacle when dust-bound leafs wash onto
sandy shores—youthful, romantic wings, castles, not
lasting a day, are testaments to eternal life:
temporary empires, composed of the
eroded walls of you, Rome,

Grace, before a meal of lightly treading thoughts is a
welcomed guest before a crashing company of waves
sinking forever into the boundless sands
below…

From "iPoems for the Dolphins to Click Home About" (2010)

Fifteen years hence, I still remember the day well. It was in my second month settling into my new life working at a non-profit based in Antigua, Guatemala. I woke up easily that morning and filled my camel pack full of water. I put my Cannon camera in my bag and strapped a machete to my belt. I set off to explore the hills surrounding my new life. I sat on a cliff-side perch above the clouds and suddenly my mind traveled beyond the immediate vista to a beach in Greece where I imagined my grandmother walking barefoot in a green skirt. The image is the image—what evokes the image isn't so easy to explain. I felt in a transcendental instant the poetry that lived in her taking life in me. I picked up my pen and the poem Seaside Grace poured onto the blank page.

My grandmother replied uncharacteristically two and a half weeks later:

> My, I had to take some time to acknowledge your latest **paean**. I blush, of course, and also am touched by your imagery, cadence, analogies - there is raw talent in your written words, an innocence blended with worldliness...I encourage more poetry, concrete as well as abstract. You have for a subject matter every exotic place you are traveling. I am doing poorly - not sleeping well, in discomfort. But grabbing as many waking hours I can to cuddle the mister, greet friends in my private quarters (I am still adhering to Emily Dickinson's "The soul reflects her own society/then shuts the door/on her divine

majority/obtrude no more."I am not unfriendly, but I need to pick my own time and protect my own space. I am writing some essays for a marketing gal - for pay! Catch us up. I assume you got your birthday funds...the check cleared here.

Love to your siblings and folks...Grandma A

That email was the first time I read that word, "Paean." Looking back a decade and a half later, I see this moment for what it was—a pivotal step on my path toward poetry. It was the first time an adult in my world had read my work and affirmed what was inarticulate within me, "There is raw talent in your written words." I am not a well-known poet, but I am a sincere one. And I sense that's all that's needed. Sincerely seeing and saying.

MY PAEANS ARE YOUR PAEANS

The poems compiled in this collection represents a poetic first for me. These are poems commissioned along the thematic lines proposed by my readers. These are the songs we sang together.

The project began towards the end of my time on a trip to Rishikesh, I put out a call on social media to my readers that I was starting a project of writing 30 reader-commissioned poems. Thirty-seven commissions came pouring in. It was an intimate exercise in trust and faith. Some readers entrusted me to write odes to their lost ones, explorations of their deepest fears, despairs, joys, and even David Bowie. For each I filled a single page. I sat in silence with my eyes closed before the empty sheet. I let their prompts fill my mind. I touched my pen to the page and the poetry that came had a life of its own. Isn't all true art channeled from beyond the individual towards the universal, the eternal. That's what I felt rereading the just-written page.

Thusly the poems came and gathered with the new days. Upon completion of the project, I sent the first drafting to the commissioner. And now, having finished each poem into a final form, I offer them back to the world in this collection.

I have chosen to include the date and place where each was written. This offers a hint to the journey they were written on. That chronology perhaps also insinuates a story of my poetic life—the initial diligence of writing a poem a day August 1-3rd, the increased inspiration of crescendoing to two poems a day August 4th, missing a day, resuming the commitment of a poem a day August 6-8th, then turning away for a week to retreat into silent meditation away from writing—and then quality and quantity in the week that follow—the chronology changes location, drops off, resumes with more fervor, continues until every commissioned poem is written. I am happy we have these poems we created together. Grateful that they all have a home in this collection.

May they mean to you what they've meant to me—more than words can say. But behind the words it's all there, perfectly expressed in ways definition defies.

PAEANS

*Dedicated to all those whose ideas and willingness
made this collection come to be.*

A BODY DRUG FREE
~Commissioned by Sierra~
August 1, Rishikesh

A room where no one interrupts you.
Where all your things are right where you left them.
No escape hatches,
no plans to move across town.
Where arguments are held gently in the hands,
worked through furrows rather than thrown through glass.

And through that window a view of a resting lake
on a spring day where fowl are left
to float and quack, enjoying this chance on Earth
without fleeing to some other season
in some other corridor of the cosmos.

Past the lake is a mountain
one day you will climb
to that smiling sanctuary
guided by the sight of snow-white peaks.

The future may well be a place of heavy steps and shaky refrains.
So store up peace for the storms that could come.
Light your candles—inhale your incense,
leave something beautiful behind for someone to find.
To pray is not to ask, but accept
this moment holding your hands
embracing,
shining upon you,
sitting beside you.
May you whisper to her,
May I never leave here again.

MAGIC LEGS

~Commissioned by Shiloh Skyy~
August 2, Rishikesh

There are some mountains you can't climb to,
but with magic legs can fly to.
It's when you're most awake you dream
of arms stretching wide enough
to embrace the world.

I know, life is not a race,
but hurry with me to the
heights of our hearts.
The mountain of caring is steep,
but worth the climb,
with views of soft valley hills
a river snakes through.
The mountain of accepting begins with rocky trails,
it's so easy to lose your way. But if you persist,
the panorama will open eyes to see what few glimpse.

And there are many more mountains
your magic legs can bring you to.
And from those heights you can
fly into dreams of cloudless days,
where the rays of your smile
warms the world the way only it can.

Do not look for me in the usual places.
My magic legs have carried me
further than most can imagine
in their rush from this to that.

Come find me.
Search for me
in the way our eyes meet
and don't break.
Find me in a smile
that says more than words.
I am climbing,
with magic legs
to unspoken heights.

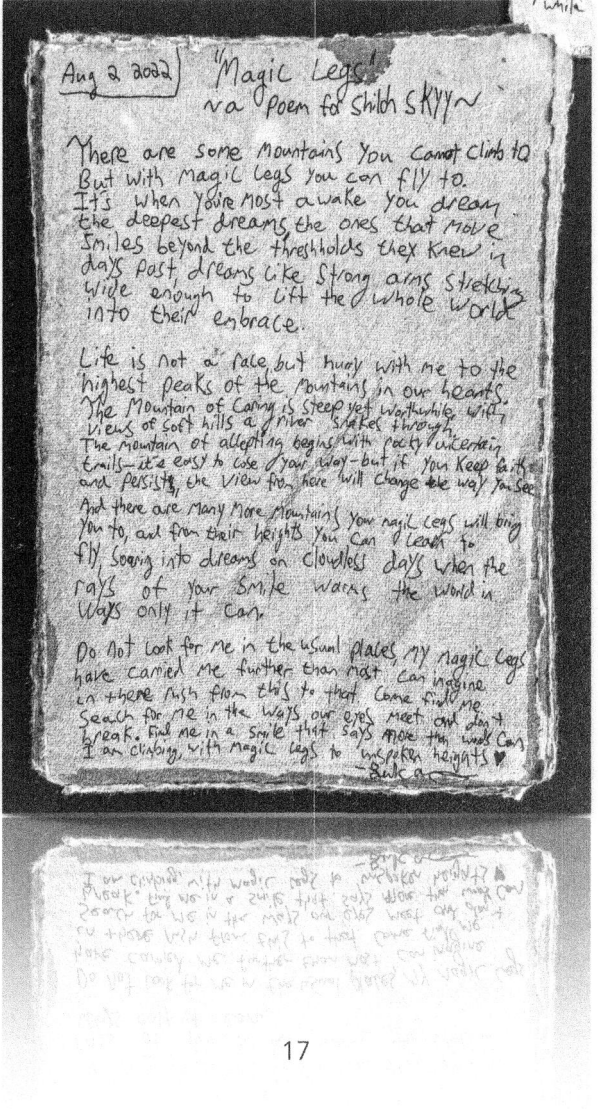

STROKE OF LUCK
~Commissioned by Chantal Van Niekirk Cotton~
August 3, Rishikesh

There's a path I used to stumble down,
off a trail I used to trip down
that leads to a pit I used to fall into,
where I'd hide and cradle my knees.

You know the place:
too many cigarettes, too much worry,
too little exercise, too much knowing
what I should be doing and too little doing it.

Then the stroke struck.
It didn't mind I was too young.
The stroke didn't care what was fair.

Sometimes it takes a flash of lightning
to illuminate a dark storm that you've felt rain down
for so long you got used to the stark weather.
But then the stroke struck–a flash and its aftermath.
The next morning I saw it all,
how I'd been and how I might be.
And I took one backward step at a time.
But you can cross great spans that way.
I cleared the trail one stone at a time,
throwing each into that dark pit within,
filling it, forgiving me, and forging a path
up the mountain I saw in the distance
I took one step towards at a time towards.

And I tell you,
worries still come, fear still calls.
Sometimes I still fall,
But I am seeing.
I am striving, even thriving.

And it's a stroke of luck when through it
you see further from the flash.
It's a stroke of unbounded fortune when
you stop making excuses and begin making good
on every promise you ever made yourself.

Here's the secret,
it's never too late to live
while you're still alive.

HOW I'LL CARRY YOU

~ Commissioned by Cindy Eyler for Ai Ozawa~
August 4, Utter Pradesh

I greeted you a thousand times hello,
but never got to say goodbye.
Still I carry those unsaid words within me,
like dishes without a sink to set them in.

You were so vibrant in life.
You taught me about joy
and so I would have wanted to see you dancing
towards what comes next.
Not sad. Not suffering.
Not afraid. Not in your forties.
You taught me about healing,
so how is it the end was like that?
How is it you who took so much suffering
out of this world could leave carrying so much?

These are the questions I must ask.
Not because they have the satisfactory answers on Earth,
but so I can get to the questions my heart needs to ask:
How will I carry you? How will your life continue in me?
How can I continue dancing to the rhythm of your life?

No, your suffering is no more.
Yes, at the appointed hour all must go.
No, I will never understand this.
Ai, there is no goodbye.
Our friendship continues,
though it's I who'll do most of the talking now.
It's easy to get caught up on the endings,
But beyond time all is a circle—birth is death and death a birth,
so I will carry the ending and the beginning and find you
sometimes smiling through my eyes
knowing in love, there is no parting.

ADVICE TO SOMEONE BUILDING A HOUSE
~A poem commissioned by Erica Derrickson ~
August 7, Almora

Start within the eyes,
your way of perceiving,
born of your way of being.
Look within and then out and around
at the way the world looks now
and imagine a distant then.
First we build a castle in the sky of imagining
then we plant a ladder in this world to reach it.

Sit still
on the place it's to be
trying to see what wants to be.

The golden ratio of our hearts is symmetry,
a you and a me,
the unyielding circle
we begin at the end
end right where we started.
Smooth out first the harsh angles
clear cluttered corners again
and turn from the enormity of the task
to each step at hand.
Dead ends open with enchantment
when you study them with a kind curiosity.
A humble dedication
untangles any knot.
Like lives, buildings are emergent.
Like art, parts and pieces become more than their sum.
Be in love with the process
because love is what builds a home.
Be unafraid of perfection,
focus joyfully and move boldly.
See the step while watching and knowing the destination.

A house is held first within the mind,
then worked out with our hands
and one day you will be surrounded
by the dream come to pass
and it will be the space that holds the body
that holds the mind
that had faith
in fantasy
that could come
to be.

MAMA BEARS

~Commissioned by Kerry Quinn about her farmstead "Mama Bears~
Aug 9, Rishikesh

I've goat to tell you about a place down in the Tennessee hills.
Where moonshiners of days past used to have a blast.
Away from it all, where a certain kind of outlaw still roams.
From garden bed to canning jars; chicken coup to goat pen;
to the pig pen where Bacon Bits eats anything you chuck him.
If you ask the pig what's goin' on,
he'll just just give you a muddy grin.
Samie the cat is too busy plotting to answer
and Chunk the Dog would rather savor the flavor
of an old shoe than entertain existential questions.

Come sit down Podner, kick off your boots and have some jam.
Let Mama Kerry serve you up something sloppy and home cooked
and tell you how love led to loss
that opened a dream from a heart seed.

That's all that's goin' on here, traveler.
Here, it's okay to be okay. Okay?
For in a rushing world, it's stillness that's golden.
In a profit food world priced to kill, it's a home-grown,
home-cooked meal that's something to savor.
In a world of tired, homesick hearts, it's the open resting hearts
who hold the havens where we remember how to stand tall
to work together to rebuild everything
slower, better, smaller.

And if that's too highfalutin for your style of tooting,
then have a taste of these pickled beets.
Anything you don't eat you can toss to the pigs.
Give Chunk a scratch on your way out
and if you fancy sittin' still and staring,
well, you might see a skunk.

RESCUE DOGS

~A poem commissioned by Lori Barnes for her rescue dogs~
August 6 ~ Bhuminadar, India

Keen, eager eyes
soft huggable body,
ever-waiting for my undivided attention.

Where people dropped the ball,
you picked it up,
brought it back to me,
so it couldn't roll too far
to find again.

Has love ever worn such untarnished white?
All dogs are service dogs employed by unconditional love.
Without qualifications, without bargaining,
without the ever unbalanced equation of human exchange.
You speak in a language of undiluted affection,
new adventure on the same path you walk every day.
Every meal is a delight.
Every day is the best day of your life.
So absorbed in enthusiasm, yet so present as to tune into
my changing weather patterns.
In Thailand they say before a soul is born a Buddha,
she is born a dog to perfect unconditional love.

They call you "rescue dogs," but I only took you in once.
You've rescued a thousand days from a lesser life.
If you are my rescue dog, I am your rescued human.

FORGIVENESS AND RESENTMENT
~ A poem commissioned by Nilda Regina Paz Marquez~
Aug 8 ~ Almora

What do the broken pieces say
to the hurling hand?
Will the hand ever know the bare foot sliced
by a shard of shattered porcelain?
Who follows a trail of red to the bedroom?
Who hears eyes sobbing for the cornered mind who holds the
hand hurting in the way of the foot
unwittingly stepping into what cuts.
Who watches the hand wipe the tears away and reach for the
broom, returning to the shattering scene to clear the path
for a better way.

See yourself as all of these:
The cup.
The hand
The blood,
The tears.
The hurting,
The hand.
The cup.
The floor, the broom and walk gently
holding yourself in softness.
See within your persecutors the tears they've yet to cry.
If you have the courage, hope for the unkindest people
in your own story to find the same embrace.
Don't do it because it's easy,
but because it will work to heal us all.
It's not easy to see the sobbing children operating weapons of
war.
But know this: They don't ever
see themselves under any true lights.
They have their reasons and you have yours,
so let go of reasons held tight by the same mind

who threw the cup and then cried for its loss.
Strive to see past all that nonsense,
straight to everyone's heart
You don't have to play in their war games,
to see the many ways the game went wrong.
The light of that vision does what the darkness cannot do.
Sometimes all a heart needs to hear is I see you and forgive you.

SANDY'S SHORE

~ A poem in remembrance of Sanford Ray White, commissioned by his loving family~
August 16 ~ Kasar Devi

The hunter's breath.
His presence.
The image of an open sky.
Soft footsteps
invisible and indivisible.
Seeing everything,
fading into the background of it all.

The muddy boots,
worn shirt.
He went out
into the world
to bring us the bounty
of this earth,
spared us
the hard work
so we could enjoy the feast.
In death as in life,
he led the way,
heading out in front
leaving us with his loss
to live
within
the memories.

We miss you,
dearest one of our hearts
our minds know
the inevitable nature of life on Earth.
But our hearts never believed in loss.

and keep the vigil for you
to return home with new quarry,
lessons we didn't realize we'd learned.

We see you everywhere,
within the breeze and bird's call.
We see you glimmer in the starlight,
glimpse you in the kindness of selfless hearts,
and in that there is no leaving,
just learning to live this new life with you
everywhere smiling from the opposite shore
of the river flowing between us,
us crying,
you laughing,
standing tall, saying,
"There is no such thing as the end."

WHY FORGIVENESS?
~A poem commissioned by Trina Challender~
Aug 16, Kasar Devi

Because you just don't know where they've been.
Because they might not either.
They might be hiding a hundred hurts behind every word.
Because night can be so utterly dark
and it's so easy to lose your way.
Because some mothers took from instead of gave to their kids.
Because some fathers simply walked out. Because some kids
were scolded for celebrating their joy, other parents couldn't afford
to feed them and no one had toys. Because we have all longed for
someone's approval and instead received their scorn. Because
you don't know who's lost what and why and some of us are
holding it all in and just barely holding on. Some wake up and hide
from the brightening day because many want to be so much more
and are devastated to watch themselves be so much less.

Because you don't know who looks back in the mirror and cringes.
And a grudge is a wall built around oneself. Life is too short to
hold onto the slights whose weight keeps us from our flight to the
light. Because why not just see the hurtful as the hurting, the
harming as the harmed, why not just let all the baggage go and
disembark the trains stuck on back and forth tracks?

In the blame game, forgiveness is the trump.
You have a monopoly called your mind if you open it.
What your fiercest oppressor cannot do is take away the light in
your eyes that looks upon all like a loving sky—infinite, warming
as the light grows, nourishing the downcast and neglected.
Forgive and be free. Then, forget you forgave
and soar into something beyond what words can say.

THINGS TO LOVE ABOUT YOU
~For Eva~
Day 5, Kasar Devi Retreat

The versions we don't know.
The you and I we may have been,
plotting and planning a surfeit of shenanigans
giggling through an apocalypse,
mayhem crafted into the shape of fun.

I love the whoever you were who set off
with a camera and backpack to India
and the way you held that glimpse and for who
and how you saw the nuance of what to notice.

The seeker in me bows to the seeker in you.
I see you, sighting good in everything,
offering what you've nourished within.
It takes a great sincerity
for the heart to trust the head
and the head to hear the heart.

I love your kindness, the way you give because
in feeding the world you are sated.

I'm glad we're meeting now
on a road where no one sees ahead.
All there is to worry about is how we walk it
and I love that we are walking it well.
I love because that is what I am.
Imagine two cartoon hearts walking down a valley road at dawn
hand in hand, happy for the moment of morning
without imagining the road ahead.

THE FALL OF FEAR
~Commissioned by Leanne Hayes~
August 16, Kasar Devi

Me? I'm ready for the Fall,
want to watch the deep green of a burning Summer surrender to
the yellows, reds, and oranges that pave the way to Winter.

Last Summer I hid
from the brightness,
evaded the crowds,
cowered beneath excuses
whose only haven is my mind.

I welcome the Winter,
love the way everything is stilled.
Not stopped, not dead; but waiting.
Hidden yet storing up stories
for seasons to come,
when everything will return fresh, anew.

I will plant
the seeds of last season's flowers,
roots entangling in the soil,
carrying the consciousness of their unmet mothers.
It happens within and without,
my eyes witness and my heart unfolds,
leaving lonely places to put myself within the flourishing of it all.

The sun warms the earth.
My heart melts her walls
 as Spring fulfills his promise again.
  newness that has never been
cycles through us again
and again
and again.

DEPRESSION'S DOOR
~Commissioned by Miriam Hagedorn Stratton~
August 19, Kasar Devi

A dark room with a closed door.
Laughter outside as
I hide beneath covers, behind curtains from a too-bright day.
Why can't I just get up and step out?
What are they saying about me?
Thoughts like broken records spin round and round.
Someone scratched the soundtrack and turned the volume
too loud and I'm feeling too small
to lift the needle and change the tune.

The doorway is quiet and still.
On the other side kids ask where their mom is.
A husband looks for his wife.
Isn't it that my friends are moving on?
How do thoughts race so quickly inside a body so still?

 And a poet answers:

There will be dark days too,
days when it feels like you're rummaging
through messy drawers, looking for a long-lost sock.
There will be fears who say the same tired things.
When there's no strength to do what might help bring some
relief, remember it's okay to feel alone and small.
There are a million shut doors
with someone hiding behind.
It's okay to be how you are today.
Hold to all that's hopeful and name the unknowns.

It's okay to ask for help and understanding.
Everyone is after feeling that spark
in the heart.
It's okay to be where you are.
Today just hold your heart with both hands
and know the sun always comes again.

MY SMILE

~Commissioned by Rebecca Jenkins ~
August 20, Kasar Devi

My smile breathes in everything.
The cold winter wind blows
into fragrant breezes of spring,
the perfume of life,
the petrichor paradise that birthed all life.

My smile is the memory of what's been
lived for and lost
hoped for but wasn't to be
the tears that reached the lips that said
what the heart wished it didn't.
Taste salt long enough and you'll long for sweetness.

When you see an elder smiling the grin of untrammeled youth,
do not assume life has been kinder in their corridor.
It might mean the wind has blown even colder,
the road rockier, the dreams in shards.
The longer you live, the more you lose.
See those radiant gray-haired smiles beaming
wonder upon the world and marvel at why.
In the answer to this is all you need to touch
the most sublime of states that comes in spite of spackles.

Hope for us all, because if you don't, there is no hope at all.
The only place that can hold such sincerity is your smile.
Seal this upon every moment,
I have seen the deepest, most indissoluble smiles emerge
from lips with the hurt, the joy, the pain, the love,
elation, sorrows and tribulations upon them.

A FALLEN TOWER
~Commissioned for Lane Bruce Tower by his brother Roger~
August 22, Kasar Devi

The image of a fallen tree in the forest,
resting below the saplings it shaded.
Still—noble—exposing new patches of sunlight to the forest floor.
The bird songs slow and careful that day,
a few clouds dare to tip-toe across the sky,
adjacent trees in awestruck wonder cast their gaze below to a
once towering tree fallen in their midst.
Of the same clutch of seeds, watered by the same rain, nourished
in the same bed of earth, connected at a million roots, flowering
together to feed the same bees, the sweetness created within
them born first in bark.

Dear world of incompressible darkness and unfathomable light,
how is it we lose our brothers?
How do we stand without falling in these winds of time and what
can we tell our mind about the blossoming secrets in our hearts?

Dear sunlight, silent and persistent, I have heard it said you still
shine atop the storms that hide the memory of you.
Life, is that you cycling through your seasons again?
Mind, why go searching for a reason when you could take refuge
in the ancestral shade where from a fallen tree a red reishi
catches the setting sun and flashes a fraternal smile as the
petrichor brings back a long lost memory.
And that's when you know it.
You are certain as one is when they glimpse truth:
we carry the candles of each other.
Like a tree we watch the small wonders
scurry through our many branches, some holding nests where
beaks not yet of this world are poised to break through to soar
within our ever-changing sky.

THE HAPPY BIRTHDAY EXPRESS
~ A poem for Mary Lou Bert commissioned by her daughter~
August 22, Delhi-Kathgodam Express

Dearest Mary,
These words fall from my pen riding the Delhi-Kathgodam
express, rolling past low pastures and their shanties,
kids playing on the tracks, rolling tires and running,
sagas appearing for just a second through my window.

I'm thinking about your eyes and the many wonders they have
seen across this country within your life that began here.
I'm thinking about the little I know about you and how yet can
picture your portrait across the bright landscape before me.
I'm thinking about the elders I have known, thinking about that
secret sealed in their smile that knows things one cannot
understand until they've lived them.

I'm imagining you hug Hathi the giant stuffed elephant who I'm told
is one of your dearest friends. I remember Hobbes, a stuffed tiger
who followed me as far as the second grade where it was time to
put stuffed animal friends away. I'm glad there comes a time again
when stuffed animals may be your dearest friends.

Happy birthday Mary Lou, from a train in India. a pilgrim is happy
to dedicate these words to you. Life, as you must know by now,
is an unexplainable mystery of divine symmetry. May your coming
year be blessed, with many small joys and delights, my pen bows
to you and Hathi as my thoughts think kindly of you.

Together for the revolution,
-Luke

WHAT MAKES ME SMILE
~*Commissioned by Jennifer Parker*~
August 22, Delhi-Kathogodam Express

Majesty of the morning.
The warmth of the tea on porcelain fingers.
Unscheduled days.
A toothless man overwhelmed by the joy of seeing me in his far-off land.
Alone in the woods.
In the woods with friends.
Early arrival to the airport.
.6mm felt tipped pens.
A bookstore.
A bigger smile if it's a used bookstore.
The biggest smile of it's a used-book shack with
piles of orphaned tomes from recently forgotten times.
Surprising people,
as noun and verb.
The Buddha. Jesus. Rumi.
Playing in a band.
Cross religious kindness.
Mutual understanding.
Hopeful perspectives.
A youthful mind seeing
a new height of possibilities.
Placing seeds in the ground.
Making the best of things.
I'm sorry. I forgive you. I love you.
The Documentary section of the of the streaming service.
Puppets. Mischief. Pranks.
Playing with the minds of the fine people of earth.
Puppets. Mischief. Pranks.
Poetry. Community. Poetic communities. Poetry communities.
Telling someone they can live by their own rules.
Puppets. Mischief. Pranks.

Sunshine. Rain. Sand.
Seeing someone pick up garbage nonchalantly from the trail.
Giving something loved away.
Looking back at all the ways it seemed things were going wrong
and seeing how everything all went right anyways.
Inspiration channeled into creation.
Dancing in the street.
Comic relief.
Comic belief.
Because life is too serious
to take so seriously.
Because ultimately what are these lives we live
but the most unlikely surprise we could have ever imagined?
Who are we in the face of our living to
paint anything but our utmost grin across each moment?

A true smile does not look past the pain
but is an act of sedition against it.
Not waiting for certain conditions,
smile from your eyes, live from your heart,
laugh from your belly.
Smile at the storms
nod to the sunny days,
place your hands in the streams
and feel blessed.
The wisest monks are laughing
the mystics of the world's great religions
are smiling a secret to each other
without anything to say.

THE RIPENING OF THE SOUL
~Commissioned for Jim Bull by his wife Myra Thompson~
August 30, Kopan Monastery

Blue poetic eyes that have watched 89 years of life.
Joyfully, curiously, ever-awed and smiling.
Joking eyes. Laughing eyes. He lived one of those lives that didn't need to be told what to do because he knew that working as a psychologist would keep him close to people his heart had the strength to serve. Free time was for prison,
to bring inmates a taste of inner freedom.
He volunteered in HIV wards
to make sure no one would die unloved and alone.
He filled his cup on hikes over forest streams, grounded his hands in garden soil, shared his thoughts with all who listened.

Once he wrote, "in order to give ourselves to the surrender of awe and wonder we need to be well grounded in the first place."

That must have been Jim's secret recipe —surrender of awe grounded in service and love—remedies to the affliction called life. This truth cannot be written on a billboard but you would have caught it in the twinkling of Jim's smile and touched it in his quick-to-help-you hands.

At the falling of these words,
as Alzheimer's allows your mind's leaves to fall gently one by one, we witness the seasons of life carry on their endless rearranging and let Jim rest.

He is such that he wouldn't have had much time to bask in our admiration or praise. He'd have asked us to help carry on his service in the world.
The only question left asking:
"What can I do today?"

SEA MOTHER
~Commissioned for Shannon Renae Grace Staska for her daughters~
August 8, Kopan Monastery

Brought to be from that deepest sea,
a mystery shrouded in the haze.
A story that tells itself as youthful hands
gathering shells upon the shore.
Imagine that cherished collection accumulating years in an attic as the things of youth are surrendered for the practices of the transition life. School dances, fleeting romances, a mother's steady gaze witnessing the changes of seasons.
So simple in the beginning.

Life grows towards increasing complications.
Amid all the variation, the constant is the loving gaze.
Seeing someone learn to walk and fall, to swim, to set out into a world of sunshine and sand, sea monsters and storms all the while broken bottles lie hidden like traps.

And the unchanging gaze,
ever hopes but is also limited
sometimes lost itself and
in an ever-decreasing lotus of control.
We watch a bloom surrender and become
then a beacon, a lighthouse,
a haven well planted, shining, steady.
We watch the changing faces of the moon,
reflected as silver blue upon the waves,
some crashing, others softly marking the shore,
a gentle touch of the Great Mother of us all,
great sea of mysteries
that on soft days you can float upon
and feel full
and free.

LOVE AT FIRST SIGHT
~Commissioned for Ginger Huie~
September 9, Kathmandu

Is it the heart swallowing the stomach
or the stomach entering the heart?
Is it future intuition
or an awareness that you'll surrender
before stepping foot on the battlefield?
What is it that stops us in our tracks?
How can someone interrupt the stream of our lives
in an unbounded instant?

Like eternity dressed as a moment in time,
like the sun shining in a puddle,
a king dressed as a commoner.
Brightness is just as blind
when you look away
everything feels dimmer.
From the gospels of the pop songs,
where we find kindred hearts
singing the song of our unbridled inclinations,
towards the someone whose name we've yet to know.

The best thing to do is nothing at all.
Is not to worry too much about the subject.
Rejoice for the mystery of hearts.
Hear within our propensity for love,
the song of all life.
It doesn't matter who flips the switch
but what is illuminated from the light.

HATS

~Commissioned by Peggy Spencer~
September 6, Kathmandu

In a basement or attic of any life
is a room filled with hats.
Some practical and protective
against life's fierce weather patterns.
Others festive—fancy—protective against life's drab.
Some keep us warm, others hide our face,
some tight, others loose, some take time to grow into.

Picture this: A grandmother's woolen snowboarding beanie
sharing a hook with the backwards baseball cap of the young
college mother hiding the hat of the teenage beauty queen—
picked up from the puddle where mean girls cast it. They weren't
real villains, just terrified by a smile that lit up the room.

Behind all that is the shawl of marriage sharing a hook with
divorce hats for sun and rain and rebirth and pain and every life is
cast to play a thousand roles where we may change our caps a
dozen times a day from bowler to beret, bonnet to boater, cowboy
to helmet cap and fez—they matter but are not so significant as
the head that holds them.
The what and why we wear means something.
Who we are matters.
How we hold our head up in a world makes a difference.
Outside eyes look first to our hats,
but few see who wears it.
Life is a mystery of being someone
whose eyes have laughed and cried,
who's gone from this to that—day to day—year to year—
and then when we set all aside and enter the inner sanctuary of
the temple where we must remove all we wear, take off our shoes
to feel in earth of that place beyond roles
where we see ourselves as a lifetime of hats
worn by a single head.

DARKNESS AS A DOORWAY
-Commissioned by Peace Mala-
September 7, Almora

There's a way to see this world
beyond black and white,
a way of being afraid without taking flight.
Shatter if you need to
into a thousand pieces
on the night floor.

Just be there in the morning,
bent over with the broom and dustpan.
Crawling too is a prostration, a supplication,
kneeling before the disasters
we are all capable of causing.

Face all your worst case scenarios.
Pick through the pile of regrets.
It's there you'll have to go to be free.
The happiest among us have seen the most pain.
They watched the winter come too early
for the spring plantings to make it.

But there are in this world ones who have walked through.
Those who waited out the winter to plant again.
Darkness is a doorway
you either walk through or into.
Only those who can tell you what they fear most
walk out to meet the spring
with more joy than makes sense
                              considering.

FINDING YOUR EMAHO
~ Commissioned for the fabulous Michelle Van Fleteron~
September 8, New Dehli

Emaho - (Tibetan) Interjection, exclamation of wonder joy and amazement at the awe of life.

When the day is difficult and you don't know where to go—Emaho!
When you're tired and hungry, wet and cold—Emaho!
When friends gather round the fire—Emaho!
Emaho in the morning.
Emaho at night.
Emaho on the foreign and domestic flights and when the other passengers give you a concerned look just throw your hands up and say, "don't you know? It's Emaho!"

Emaho in the mountains.
Emaho on the beach.
Emaho in the swamps infested with leaches.
Emaho your friends.
Emaho those who broke your heart
and didn't pick up any of the pieces.
Emaho this moment, for it will never come again!
Emaho when you wake and say Emaho! as you drift off to sleep
Emaho all you regret—don't worry—don't fret—it doesn't matter how you spent the last 30 years.
Emaho this day.
Emaho this life.
Emaho your dog and the most minuscule things because it doesn't matter what you have or who you know, or if your teeth glow or your dog knows how to sit or if you keep your job or quit,
all that really matters is how you Emaho!

THEIR VOICE

~Commissioned by Sally Newberry for the Sēn Rescue Sanctuary~
September 8, New Delhi

Dogs left to the side of the road
abandoned farm animals, discarded, voiceless, choice-less.
Pleading for someone to take note of their plight.
It is those beings, human and animal, who cannot ask for help
or help themselves who are those who most need it.

Yet there are in this world eyes that see
and hands who lift the discarded out of the ditches and gutters
to a place where they can be part of this world again.
The key is not to get lost in the scope and scale of the calamities,
but to see that for every sad story is a diligent helper
working to re-write these stories, twisting the tragedies into the
happy new beginnings that emerge
before the story stopped being told at all.

This a world of sanctuaries too.
This is also a world of heroes and havens.
It's a place of fresh starts and artful living.
There is recovery here too.
So see the miseries to understand the mystery
of why some avoid the unseemly sights
and others race towards them,
unafraid and willing to do what needs to be done.
So dogs can play, lamas frolic, cats creep, goats giddy-up
and a human heart blooms in the joy that comes
from being a someone who works from the heart
for all hearts, who cares and carries
those left on fringes to the freedom of a fresh start.

THE MOUNTAIN'S GAZE
~*A poem Commissioned by Lauren Busing*~
September 8, New Delhi

Staring to a distant peak- *Annapurna, Everest, Machu Picchu,*
Lhotse, Makalu and *Meru*— *Denali* and *Diablo,*
What is this sentiment they stir?
It takes lifetimes to answer.
Eyes climb the landscape to the spire in the sky,
older than everything.
How every generation before
must have stopped and stared,
fixated for an eternal moment
upon the most unchanging thing on this earth.
Wearing the garments of the season, suffering snows and rains,
unmoved amid forest fires, a firm place to put our minds
in this transient realm of earth, the human animal scurrying
upon the high wires, hiding nuts,
finding a burrow where to rest.
Mountains watching the play of life.
Primordial cathedrals, castles, keeps for our heart.
Eminent pinnacles grounded below,
reaching from their base to touch the night of stars.
"Live," I swear they whisper, "like you will lose everything."

HOW TO BE AT PEACE IN THE WORLD
~ *A Poem Commissioned for Janis Garren Ryberg*~
September 8, New Delhi

When you see suffering,
see if you can lend a hand.
When you witness unkindness,
see if you can find understanding.
For it too is a suffering that goes
unseen in our darkest places—
places we don't admit we know the way to.
Walk gently to sing fully to live kindly
to leave everyone with more dignity
than you found them with.
Practice patience,
accept what you can't change.
The world is a place of rocks
unmoved for eons.
You are capable and in motion.
With strength and time to move stones.
But only a few of the many
so choose carefully
where and what and why.

Wisdom sees what efforts would be wasted.
The right piece of gravel, moved at the right time,
may start a landslide.
So choose wisely where you walk
what you reach for and why.
Change yourself and the whole world is recast.
Everything you do matters as much as you mean it.

FAITH. DOUBT. AND COURAGE IN MEDITATION.
~ A Poem commissioned by Maureen Schou Bornstein~
September 9, New Dehli

The reasons why not can't meet
the eyes of why.
There's always something so important to do
in the unending maintenance of life and sitting still
sometimes feels like serving hard time.
Left unearthed the mind will wander to anywhere but here.
Who truly knows the place,
who has had the time to settle
into where we run from?

We race down the paths we've been shown,
we ride congested rails,
traffic moving away or toward things, never into them.
But there's a dusty trail you have to believe in to find,
an avenue that goes past all the reasons
to keep the pace of humanity's race.
There is a prod from a mountain by which singing springs are
serenading the impulse to take the first steps.

The business of the world is endless.
If you wait today do you think a new tomorrow will ever dawn?
Doubts are endless, so you'll have to learn to live with them.
It's easy to run through this world.
It takes great courage to stop and look around.

To see all you hope to see,
you'll have to turn and face all you wished not to see.
But hold faith in the face of doubt. Courage is coursing in you.
It's easy to travel the earth,
rare are those who travel beyond it while within it.

All you need to do is
take a seat
and look
at what comes
with care,
determination,
curiosity,
and kindness.

Faith finds its footing in doubt.
Courage is fed by the flames of fear.
They carry you further than you imagine
if you don't listen to all that would keep you underground,
where they tell only stories in the shadows of a great light.

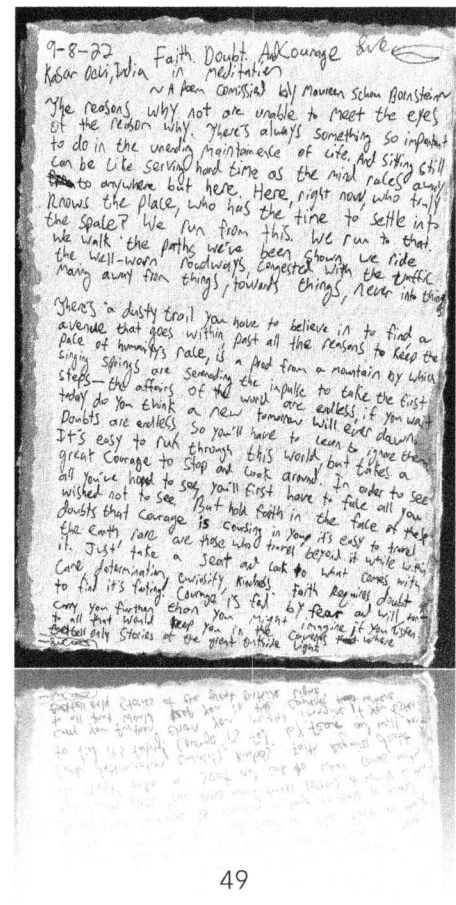

SEEING THE SEA
~Commissioned for Hershel Ben Snow by Goldie Roberts~
September 8, New Delhi

There's an image we all know
of an old man staring out towards a stormy sea.
The wind skids across the tops of waves.
A wolf colored sky sprinkles rain, the prelude to the coming show
of lightning backed by an orchestra of thunder
playing the greatest theater on earth.

And the old man just stares.
And sometimes you are the man and sometimes the staring eye
and sometimes you contemplate the mystery of the sea and
sometimes you contemplate the mystery of that man who stares
stoically to the mother of all life.
The sea is a verb, a universe, creator and destroyer.
We cast a fishing line into her like rolling the dice of destiny.

As you empty the vessel of thought,
you become the observer of this poetic instant
of an old man who stares out to the sea at a speck of a ship on
the horizon, where a baby is born, who will one day find a hermit
crab's home, abandoned on the sands
a seafood wind blows across.
Pelicans glide in their grace
over the crest of a wave, carrying a surfer,
who doesn't know he's practicing zen.
Children oblivious to the tidal schedule build castles
that house a future of dream,
glimpsed by lovers walking barefoot,
arm in arm, towards the setting sun eclipsed by a scene of
atavistic seagull soaring
in and out to the fading rhythm of a star-born night.
Let these lines of verse lead you to deepen into the sea
of your own mind, as mysterious and profound
as any ocean on earth.

BALANCE IN THE CHAOS
~A poem commissioned by Jen Goldman~
September 15, Bismarck

The twinkling of a thousand lights,
possibilities playing across the mind.
Too hurried to stay.
Leaving before you've arrived
in this life of this way or that.
We consume until we're consumed
by the silence we never knew.

Behind all the motion there is still a stillness.
Amid all the commotion there is a quiet corner,
Off a side street in an alley, is a seat where the longer you sit the
fewer reasons you'll have to leave.
Set down your bags, cancel your plans and breathe.
They say hidden in each inhale is a little edge of eternity.
In every exhale, anything lost can be found.

Look at your life from your smile.
Look after your mind with the patient determination
that leads the wildness of a colt
into the wisdom of the loyal stead.

Lead yourself to spring fed fields.
Caress your long face,
rub your forehead tenderly,
see with eager eyes.
Diving into glacial waters
that cool upon crossing to the island in the middle of the rush.
Here you can rest and find the pulse of spring
preparing for yet another unfolding.
All around—life is happening—
and you are within it, crossing its currents
without being swept away, inhaling all that is
to exhale all that will be.

INDECISION

~A poem commissioned by Brandy Lee Harrison~
September 17, Bismarck

The thousand avenues of thought a mind may meander down.
The many ways to pace through days,
back and forth, weaving five-dimensional patterns in time.

Imagine a new spring day with someone singing in your kitchen
a song you think you know.
Dust dances within columns of light,
a sizzle emits a scent of burning butter.
And that's when you lose yourself
within the many ways to use up the day.
So many directions and their outcomes.
Music on a radio,
I set my life to shuffle,
check my phone again,
look for purpose in the fridge.

To choose not to choose
is the perishable choice.
Tell me where is life alive and sunburned?
Who manages to see clearly
through these fogs?
There's so many ramps and sidetracks,
shortcuts and routes running through dreams
with off-ramps every mile into nightmares,
where you gotta keep moving
to keep the monsters behind you.

In the end, it won't matter so much what you did,
but how you did it.
The only gift that's worth giving
is your utmost.
If you're unsure how to do that

know there's an art to the waiting.
If you feel lost,
then a new journey back home
must be waiting.

Stare in the face of these fears
and see if you can make them smile.
When in doubt at what to do,
just stand in wonder of it all.
Brew something warm and inviting
and let the sunlight rest on your face.
It's traveled so far to be here.
Let it in to remind you that
everything alive
orbits an inner life orbiting
a brightness beyond what we understand.

GROUND CONTROL TO DAVID BOWIE
~Commissioned for David Bowie by Elizabeth Froelicher~
September 17, Bismarck

Dear David Bowie,

I have been commissioned to write this poem about you and my
initial thought was, "Who the hell is David Bowie?
Yes, I'd heard your name many times and had a vague notion
as to who you were, but had never really asked,
"Who is David Bowie?"
So I put on your music whiling reading your Wikipedia
and when my m research revealed you were no longer alive,
I sighed. Sorry about that Mr. Bowie.
Mr Bowie, the more I learn of your legend, the more I wish I wasn't
so late to this party. As you sing on my Spotify, I'm hearing songs I
know but didn't KNOW. You know?

What I hear is hard rock fed a strict diet of mangos
on a plush bed stuffed with a lusty curiosity for life.
I hear frequent searching the stars for melodic mellow dramas.
It's snappy. Joyous is the sound. Rock in soft silk socks.
A dragon cuddling a puppy. NASA'S musical spinoff.
When Aliens come, you bet you'll be on the playlist (if they came
to party). If they come to destroy, we'll blare Starman
as everything burns down around.

Ground control to Major Tom, Mr. Bowie, are you in?
It's Mr. Mercury calling, forgot his sunglasses on Mars and he's
wondering if you can swing by and grab them on your next flyby?

My invocation for you David is: may your music take the future
with you on journeys beyond the drab days.
This time let's not go to Mars. Let's find a current in the solar wind
and sail it to the edge of the possibility your music dances upon.

LOVE OF LIFE

~Commissioned by Rosemary Tarof for Michael and Emily~
September 19, Bismarck

Cheat the system: Pay off student loans
doing something you love.
Enlist in the navy,
but sail the inner sea.
See the most hardened faces of humanity and come back
to shore with a grin that smiles from having seen a thousand
roads untaken because they led away from the light.

No one can stop you, you know, from dancing like you like to.
Not from singing what you want to, from living as you wish to.
No one can keep you from your commitment
to recovering innocence lost.
No one can prevent you, from dreaming of those mountains you're
capable of conjuring and hiking to horizons one step at a time.

Fly away dear one, because so many are
trapped in the mud and only by flying will you soar and
see from above the view that glimpses us all.
Just never forget where you forged those wings,
made from so many moments woven together.

Remember you don't need to move a muscle only shift the attitude
to make your world a place where you've nothing to prove
and everything to celebrate and elevate.
Life is on your side,
and there's nothing she will not
do for her fans and lovers.

THROUGH A CHILD'S EYE
~Commissioned by Charlene Elias~
September 19, Bismarck

Approach the grasshopper slowly,
keep the spot where it lands ever in mind.
Let this moment consume your world.
A feline approach towards compounding eyes
that sees a single image from a thousand facets of perspective,
each as fascinating as the next.
Then a moment of utter totality.
The universe takes a deep breath,
neither grasshopper nor child moves.
Then everything returns,
there's a sprint and careful hands surround six legs
as jubilant fingers hold the quarry up
 with unbounded delight.
Think not lightly of this image,
but turn to it over and over again
to discover how some carry an
opulent and unassailable enchantment
while others succumb to the swamps
and bogs of growing up.
As a child knows well:
as some grow taller their hearts grow smaller.

The question worth most asking is
How do I run towards my life
as that child races
towards the grasshopper of his boundless desires?
Where do we lose that?
How can we regain it?

The world is as we see it.
We are as we see ourselves within it.
Don't let these be more mere words,
let these be the path through the

locked-up elations
you once immersed yourself in daily.

The world is ever-wafting as much
awe as she's had.
The story of disenchantment is a fiction
written by our minds.
So why not let your walk through life
be a secret dance from joy to joy?
Why not be someone with wonder filling each breath.
There's nothing childish about looking with a child's eyes.
In fact, it might be the bravest thing
considering
the dying logs
lodged in so many paths.

COCOON STAGE
~Commissioned for Tammy Clark ~
September 25, Bismarck

It's what moves the legs to take a
thousand steps towards destiny,
Something like a desire for truth.
With each bite the appetite grows
until it reaches a size beyond which it can't continue.
On the edge of a barren branch, alone.
No longer surrounded by hungry brothers and sisters,
she's a survivor of sorts.
She's one who cannot live as she's lived anymore.
Metaphor of metaphors, a fable told through life's seasons;
it's the story of from nothing and no one, to birth and hunger,
to consuming and getting by while changing.
Then suddenly you wake from sleep winged and soaring
above the hungry life you once lived below,
where you kept to your cravings
and hid beneath a moldy leaf.

Inside the cocoon everything was fluid and flowing.
After all your organs dissolved, you were sure you were dead.
You met your Creator, and she was a giant tree.
And from that primordial stew, something that felt like you stirred.
And so it was, a butterfly deer-walked out of the chrysalis and
neatly unfolded her wings. Meek as monarch, bright as a
swallowtail, unseen, like the star glass eyes of the buckeye—
so unlikely the way of things.
Lift your eyes to this beaming truth of life
to fill your mind with the wildest of imaginings.
Somewhere within each insatiable worm is the urge to
leave the hungry world behind and take flight.

ALSO ANXIETY
~Commissioned by Miriam Stratton~
September 25, Bismarck

Why is it wherever I go, whatever I do
some disaster seems lurking?
Anxious for others' anxiety.
Afraid of another's fear.
How to support others without tripping over them?
What is it we're all afraid of?
Who is the unseen silhouette blowing
ominous smoke rings around every bend?

My mind is still a hunter-gatherer,
trying to find a safe tree of nourishing fruits—
maybe a mate, a stick to scratch my back, shelter from the storms,
a place I don't need to hide in or run from.
How do you kiss anxiety away?
Tenderly.
How to teach fear to fly away?
Patiently.

What could go wrong, might also go all right.
It's never what I'm afraid of,
but the thought that I might never
still myself long enough to stare it in the eyes.
Resist the thought you have to face it all alone.
You don't. And you won't. Because you can't.
So tell your worries to be worried.

Tell your fears that you are going to tell everyone about them.
Watch how they shrink and fade.
It's okay to feel caught in a worried wind,
anxious breezes blow around all over town.
Just keep your feet planted and when it passes
you will be what's standing stronger
for having stood straight in one of life's storms.

THE NEXT CHAPTER
~Commissioned for Cynthia Church Parker~
September 25, Bismarck

Some days
I want to throw the book of life
out of the vehicle.
I become so tangled in a particular plot line and
never understand why the story is told with so much suffering.
What's the point of so much difficulty along the way?
What hearts seek is the knowing
it's all worth something.
For life to matter, we must become
the character we believe we might yet be.

When you can't rewrite the story,
focus on character development.
Beyond what is told around us,
we can see what keeps us from flaring our inner light.
We can be one who was misshaped by the plot twists
or one who contorted their spirit to escape
in spite of conditions that might have kept you bound.
Some days I want to put down the book of life and pick up a good
fantasy to lose myself like a forest of trees disappearing into a fog.
And it's from here I turn back before I stray too far.
As I near the edge, something certain emboldens my winged heart
and I remember I also have feet made to walk the Earth.
I turn to new pages, because once the story has you,
you continue to trudge through it.
I hold the weather beaten tome, read a new chapter,
and am willing to fall in love with my story again.

SUNFLOWER IN THE CONCRETE
~Commissioned by Elizabeth Sparks for a Sunflower in the Road~
September 25, Bismarck

Close your eyes and imagine:
A sunflower opening its rays from the asphalt.
A crack in the concrete on the side of a road
shoulders a remote possibility.
How are you reading this with your eyes closed?

No one told the seedling
of the long odds of a kernel
buried in concrete.
All it had was
faith that where the sunlight beckoned
life would follow.
Alive in the dank and dark,
it emerged
That's just what life does—lives.

And when you see life living like that,
stop and make the sign of the cross,
or namaste,
or bow,
or offer a prayer up to your greatest doubts.
This is our story:
we bloom in spite all that would deprive us.
My heart is a flower tracking the sun,
adjusting to the perfect angle to receive the most light.

In the sheerness of this simplicity
you find better results than
all the complicated strategies
for finding the light.

The lesson is:
In the darkness wait,
keep hope alive,
the future is unwritten.
Seek the light
regardless of circumstance
or situation.
When a crack opens, use all you can muster
to push through it.
Don't worry about all that might crush you,
rise or miss the chance forever.
When it's time—bloom!
Blossom dear one, even if you bloom alone.
This is between you and the light.
And if you one day begin to resemble the sun,
keep the humble memory of the seed always in hand.
You who grew to fill a moment and became a new source of life,
this poem is a petal
that began beneath a scorching July road.
Your eyes are petals too,
unfolding from an undying bloom
into a living life.

ABOUT THE AUTHOR AND KOKO BEAR

Before the age of two, **Koko Bear's** activities are shrouded in mystery. Did he once have another family? Was he always a street dog? Who the hell taught him how to play banjo like that?

Legend has it Koko roved with the Chimichuri Circus, preforming parlor tricks in the seven rings before escaping after developing a fear of jumping through the flaming hoop. As no one's ever seen him jump through a flaming hoop, everything verifiable in this story checks out. He likes to watch butterflies, is an avid fan of chasing games, LOVES treats! and doesn't like it when people walk by.

Author Luke Maguire Armstrong is happy you've reached this point of the page and read the preceding paragraph. He hopes you didn't become triggered and skip ahead. If you did, it is his strong desire that you go back and re-read Koko's bio. Beyond that, he doesn't know what else to say, although he thinks writing in the third person is fun, if not somewhat tongue-in cheek.

From the hammock, he thanks you. From the road, he beckons you to see. To the sky, he marvels. In a cup of tea, he finds more than enough. In gratitude to you dear reader, he rests. Thank you for reading and being part of these poetic possibilities. See you around the next poetic bend. —LMA

SPECIAL THANKS TO

All those who heeded the call and commissioned poetry. Thanks to my friends in copy editing, Daithi Neavyn, Miel, Elizabeth and Steve Sparks. Thanks to my grandmother for the word "Paeans" and all the words. To my dear readers who bring the art of my heart into the full circle. To the poets and artists of Karuna for the echo chamber of inspiration. Thank you the moon for her 3am calls.

OTHER WORKS BY AUTHOR INCLUDE:

Amazing Grace for Survivors (2008)

iPoems for the Dolphins to Click Home About (2010)

How We are Human (2012)

Bushwick Poetry (2013)

Her Life on Paper (2014)

The Nomad's Nomad (2014)

All the Beloved Known Things (2018)

The Starlight Still Within Us (2021)

How One Guitar Will Save the Word (2021)

Voices of the Valley: Poetea Collection (2022)

The Upwards We Could Still Climb (2022)

Original Music: http://alekoshatitlan.bandcamp.com

Printed in Great Britain
by Amazon